Marco
He's a jo[ker], messing [...] always m[...] if he som[...] things wrong.

Waxy Max
He's very sporty and football mad. On the outside, he's tough, but underneath he's got the biggest heart.

Philippa Feltpen
A real peacemaker, she helps keep the other Pens in order by sorting out arguments and giving good advice.

Splodge, we're going canoeing!

Squiggle and Splodge
The Scribble twins! They're both quiet, both shy. Although they may not look alike, they do almost everything together.

Enter ...

"Let's have some fun, Splodge!"

"Yes, please, Squiggle!"

Pens
Helping you to get to know God more

Yes God!

Written by Alexa Tewkesbury

Every day a short Bible reading is brought to life with the help of the Pens characters. A related question and prayer apply this to daily life. Written in four sections, two focusing on the lives of Pens and two on Bible characters, young children will be inspired to learn more of God and His Word.

What's inside?

- **Obeying God** — Day 1
- **Elisha's Instructions – When Naaman said yes** — Day 10
- **God's Invitation** — Day 16
- **A Great Feast – Who's coming to the party?** — Day 25

CWR

Mixed Sources
Product group from well-managed forests and other controlled sources
www.fsc.org Cert no. SGS-COC-003963
© 1996 Forest Stewardship Council

Day 1

OBEYING GOD

'LORD, you have given us your laws and told us to obey them faithfully.' (Psalm 119 v 4)

A special week

'Is everybody listening?' asked Miss Fountain Pen.

All the little Pens in the classroom stopped talking. Except Henry Highlighter.

'*I'm* listening, Miss,' Henry chattered. 'You're listening, too, aren't you, Squiggle and Splodge? And you, Rowena. We're all listening.'

'Next week at school will be very exciting,' announced Miss Fountain Pen. 'We're going to be doing some special activities. So you must all make sure that you do exactly as you're told. That way, you'll stay safe and have lots of fun, too.'

'I *always* do as I'm told, don't I, Miss?' chirped Henry.

'Almost always, Henry,' smiled Miss Fountain Pen.

Just as teachers want us to obey them, God wants us to obey Him, too.

What 'special activity' could you do this week?

Pens Prayer

Dear Lord, please help me always to do as You want me to. Amen.

Day 2: Obeying God

'… I will study your teachings. Your instructions give me pleasure …' (Psalm 119 vv 23–24)

The best instructions

On Monday morning, Miss Fountain Pen said, 'Today, we're going to make models with clay.'

She showed Pens how to mould the clay into different shapes.

Henry was very excited. 'I'm making a clay dog,' he chuckled.

But he was in such a hurry that his dog didn't look very dog-like at all.

'Slow down, Henry,' smiled Miss Fountain Pen.

So, slowly, Henry started again.

When his dog was finished, Squiggle laughed, 'Brilliant, Henry! It looks just like Sharpy!'

'That's because I did what Miss Fountain Pen said,' smiled Henry proudly. 'Miss Fountain Pen's instructions are the best!'

God wants us to do as He asks because He wants the best for us.

If you had some Playdough (or clay), what would you make?

Pens Prayer

Father God, thank You for speaking to me through the Bible. Amen.

Day 3 — Obeying God

'In the night I remember you, LORD, and I think about your law.' (Psalm 119 v 55)

Too excited!

On Monday night, Henry was so excited that he couldn't sleep.

'Tomorrow, we're going canoeing!' he whispered to himself. 'I've never been canoeing before. Miss Fountain Pen says we have to wear special jackets called buoyancy aids. They'll help us to float if the canoe tips over and we fall in the water. And Miss Fountain Pen says I've got to sit still in the canoe and not get too excited.'

Henry giggled. 'The trouble is,' he added, 'I'm too excited already! But I'm going to remember Miss Fountain Pen's instructions. I want to try to do everything just right.'

God's instructions to us are written in the Bible. Thinking about them helps us remember them.

Can you think of any of God's instructions to us?

Pens Prayer

Thank You, Lord God, for loving me. I want to spend time with You every day. Amen.

Day 4 — Obeying God

'How I love your law! I think about it all day long.'
(Psalm 119 v 97)

Boating Pens

On Tuesday morning, Henry squealed, 'Canoeing today!'

Down by the river, the little Pens put on their buoyancy aids.

Henry helped them. 'Buoyancy aids will help us float if the canoe tips over,' he explained sensibly. 'Miss Fountain Pen says so. And we must sit still in the canoe and not get too excited.'

'Well done, Henry,' Miss Fountain Pen beamed. 'You've remembered everything I told you.'

Then she sat in the big canoe with the little Pens, and rowed them all along the river.

'I *am* too excited,' thought Henry, 'but I'm not going to forget to sit very still.'

It makes God happy when we follow His instructions.

What do we call the long paddles that are used to row a boat?

Pens Prayer

Loving Lord, please help me to remember what I read about You in the Bible. Amen.

Day 5 — **Obeying God**

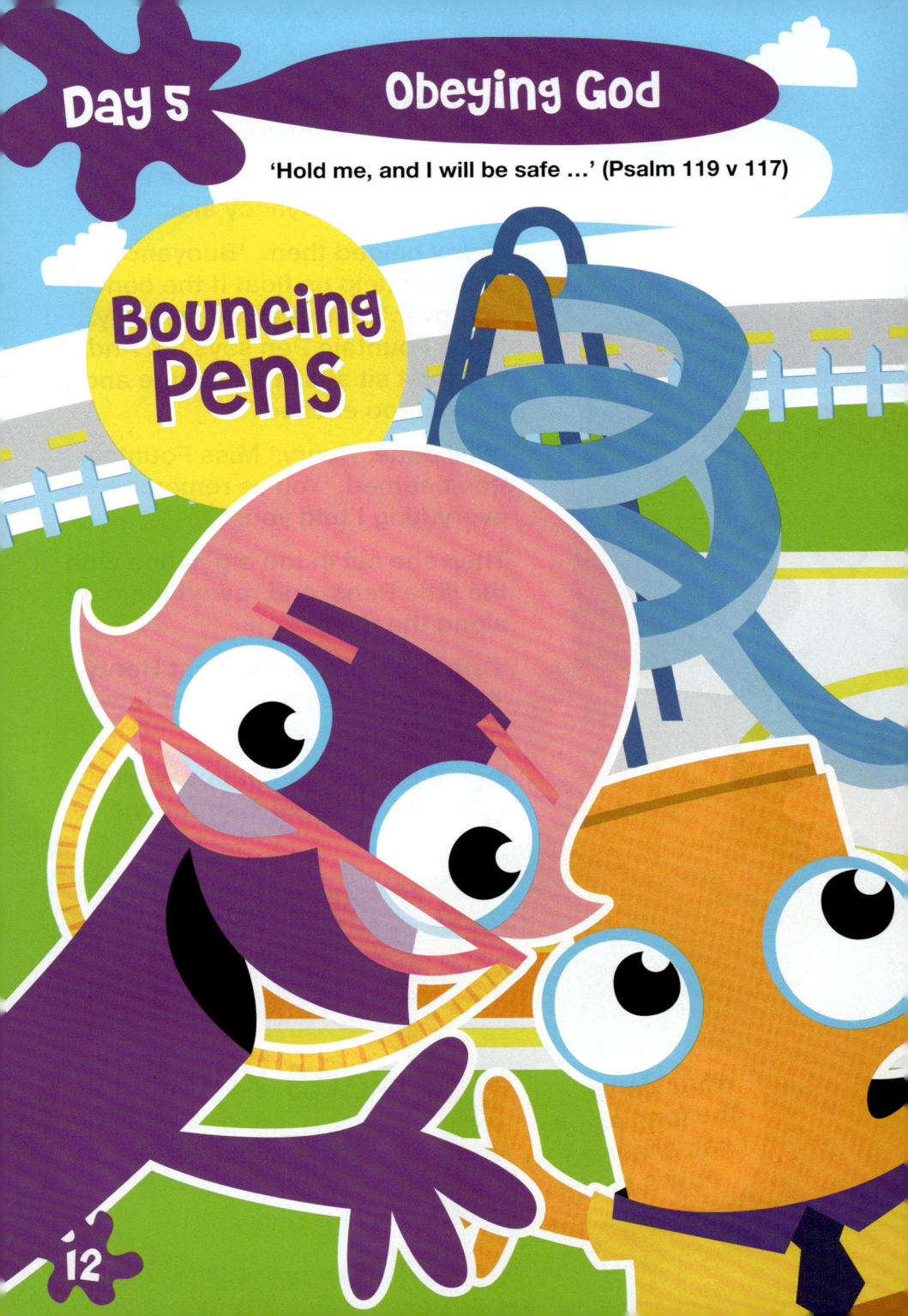

'Hold me, and I will be safe …' (Psalm 119 v 117)

Bouncing Pens

On Wednesday morning, Miss Fountain Pen announced, 'Today, little Pens, you're going to bounce on a trampoline.'

'Wow!' squealed Squiggle and Splodge.

'Cool!' laughed Rowena Rollerball.

'Hooray!' cheered Henry.

But inside, Henry wasn't sure he felt like cheering. When he saw how high Splodge could bounce, all he felt was scared.

'You'll stay here while I'm bouncing, won't you, Miss Fountain Pen?' Henry mumbled.

'You don't have to bounce any higher than you want to, Henry,' said Miss Fountain Pen kindly. 'And of course I'll stay. We're all here to help each other.'

One of God's instructions to us is to trust Him.

Can you think of any animals that bounce?

Pens Prayer

Father God, teach me to trust You the way You want me to. Amen.

13

Day 6 — Obeying God

Games

'… give me understanding, so that I may know your teachings.' (Psalm 119 v 125)

Little drummer Pens

On Wednesday afternoon, Miss Fountain Pen said, 'Time to do some drumming, little Pens!'

Henry was in a group with Squiggle, Splodge and Rowena. They each had a drum and were trying to play a rhythm.

'No, Henry,' said Rowena. 'You're getting the rhythm wrong.'

'Let's count,' suggested Squiggle. 'I'll bang my drum when we count "one". Splodge can bang hers on "two", Rowena on "three" and Henry on "four".'

The little Pens counted and banged their drums – and they played their rhythm perfectly.

'I got it right!' beamed Henry. 'I understand what I'm supposed to do now.'

God uses other people to help us understand what He teaches in the Bible.

Can you make up a rhythm by clapping your hands?

Pens Prayer

Dear God, help me to learn something new about You this week. Amen.

Day 7 — Obeying God

'As you have promised, keep me from falling …'
(Psalm 119 v 133)

Climbing Pens

On Thursday morning, Miss Fountain Pen said, 'Today, we're going to an activity centre to climb a climbing wall!'

'Hooray!' shouted Henry.

But when they arrived, he suddenly felt nervous.

'It's a very high wall,' he frowned. 'What if I fall?'

'You can't fall,' smiled Miss Fountain Pen. 'You'll be held with a strong rope.'

When it was Henry's turn to climb, he still looked worried.

'The rope *is* strong enough to hold me, isn't it?' he mumbled.

'That rope has held all your friends,' nodded Miss Fountain Pen. 'You can be sure it will hold you, too.'

God has promised that He will never let us go.

Can you think of any other promises God has made?

Pen's Prayer

Lord God, thank You that You always keep Your promises to us. Amen.

Day 8 — Obeying God

'I obey your commands and your instructions; you see everything I do.' (Psalm 119 v 168)

Dancing Pens

On Friday morning, Miss Fountain Pen said, 'Today, little Pens, you're going to dance! Listen to the music, and pretend you're plants growing in a garden.'

The music played and the little Pens' dance began.

Some were trees and stretched up tall.

Others were flowers. They waved their hands like leaves and petals moving in the wind.

'I'll be a snail,' Henry giggled, 'and I'll eat up all the flowers!'

'Don't be silly, Henry,' called Miss Fountain Pen. 'What can you be, growing in the garden?'

'Erm …' wondered Henry. Then he smiled – and decided he'd be an apple tree.

God sees everything we do – and He hopes we'll do as He asks us to.

Who can you ask to help you obey God?

Pens Prayer

Dear Lord, I'm sorry for times when I do things You don't want me to do. Please help me to do right things, not wrong things. Amen.

Day 9 — Obeying God

'I wander about like a lost sheep; so come and look for me, your servant …' (Psalm 119 v 176)

Pens go walking

On Friday afternoon, Miss Fountain Pen announced, 'Now for the last activity of our activities week. We're going for a walk – and we'll find our way by using a map.'

'Whoopee!' yelled Henry. He was feeling very excited again. 'Who wants to *walk*, though? Not me. I'm going to *race* you!'

'Henry, no!' said Splodge. 'We must stay together. Then Miss Fountain Pen can help us find the right way.'

'Without Miss Fountain Pen, Henry,' agreed Squiggle, 'you know that you'll only get lost.'

'I suppose,' sighed Henry. 'And anyway,' he grinned, 'I'd probably just be lonely by myself.'

When we stay close to God, our Friend, He will lead and guide us.

Have you ever seen a map? Why are maps so useful?

Pens Prayer

Father God, I want to live the way You want me to. Thank You that Jesus shows me how. Amen.

ELISHA'S INSTRUCTIONS
When Naaman said yes

Day 10

'Naaman … was a great soldier, but he suffered from a dreaded skin disease.' (2 Kings 5 v 1)

The brave soldier

Naaman was an important man. He was the commander of the army in a country called Syria. The king of Syria was very pleased with him. His soldier, Naaman, had won lots of battles.

But Naaman was sad. He was ill with a horrible disease. There were sore patches all over his skin.

Naaman might be the greatest solider – but no one could make him better.

Not even the king of Syria could find someone to help Naaman.

Who helps you when you're ill?

Pens Prayer

Lord God, when I know someone's not feeling well, please help me to be kind to them. Amen.

Elisha's Instructions
When Naaman said yes

Day 11

'… the prophet who lives in Samaria … would cure [Naaman] of his disease.' (2 Kings 5 v 3)

The servant girl

Naaman's wife had a servant. She was only a young girl. Naaman's army had taken her from her home in Israel. Now she worked in Naaman's house in Syria.

The servant girl knew how ill Naaman was. She knew that no one in Syria could help him.

So, one day, she went to her mistress and said, 'There is a man in Israel who could make Naaman well again. His name is Elisha and he serves God. God gives him the power to make ill people better.'

The servant girl was sure that God would use Elisha to make Naaman better.

What work do you think the servant girl had to do?

Pens Prayer

Dear Father, help me to tell other people about Your love and Your power – just like the servant girl. Amen.

Elisha's Instructions
When Naaman said yes

Day 12

'Send the man to me, and I'll show him that there is a prophet in Israel!' (2 Kings 5 v 8)

Naaman goes to Israel

26

Naaman wasn't one of God's friends yet. But when he heard about God's servant, Elisha, he wanted to go to Israel to find him. So the king of Syria wrote a letter for Naaman to give to the king of Israel, telling him who Naaman was, and asking him to make Naaman better.

Then Naaman set off on his journey.

When he arrived, the king of Israel read the letter.

'Oh dear,' he frowned. 'How can I make this man well? I'm not God.'

But Elisha sent him a message: 'Tell Naaman to come and see me.'

Elisha knew that God wanted him to help Naaman, so he obeyed Him.

Do you know someone who isn't friends with God yet? Talk to God about them now.

Pens Prayer

Thank You, Lord God, for Elisha, whose story teaches me to obey You. Amen.

Elisha's Instructions
When Naaman said yes

Day 13

'Elisha sent a servant out to tell [Naaman] to go and wash himself seven times in the River Jordan …' (2 Kings 5 v 10)

Elisha sends a message

28

Naaman went straight to Elisha's house. But, when he got there, Elisha didn't come out and meet him. He just sent a servant with a message.

'Elisha says,' the servant began, 'that you must go down to the River Jordan. There, you must wash yourself in the water seven times. Do that and you'll be better.'

Naaman was angry. He was an important man. Why couldn't Elisha be bothered to come out and talk to him?

'Isn't Elisha even going to pray for me?' Naaman shouted. 'Well, I'm not jumping in the River Jordan! It's too dirty!'

When Naaman said no to Elisha, he was saying no to God, too.

How do you think God felt when Naaman wouldn't do as He wanted him to?

Pens Prayer

Loving Lord, when You ask me to do something, I want to be ready to say yes! Amen.

Elisha's Instructions
When Naaman said yes

Day 14

'[Naaman's] servants … said, "… why can't you just wash yourself, as he said, and be cured?"' (2 Kings 5 v 13)

seven dips

30

Some of Naaman's servants were with him outside Elisha's house.

One of them said nervously, 'But, sir, if Elisha had told you to do something difficult, you would have done it. Well, washing in the river is so easy. Please try it,' the servant added. 'It might make you better.'

Naaman still looked cross. But off he went to the river. He dipped down into the water – once. Twice. Three, four, five and six times.

His skin looked exactly the same.

'Nothing's happening,' he grumbled. So he dipped down for the seventh time.

Naaman washed in the river, but he didn't really believe that he'd get better.

Who trusted God? Naaman or Elisha?

Pens Prayer

Father God, please help me to trust in You. Amen.

Elisha's Instructions
When Naaman said yes

Day 15

'[Naaman] ... said, "Now I know that there is no god but the God of Israel ..."' (2 Kings 5 v 15)

Only one God

Naaman bobbed up out of the river for the seventh time. But this time, he didn't grumble. This time, he gasped!

He stared down at his hands and his arms. He gazed at the skin on his body. All the sore patches were gone! He looked healthy again. After all this time, he was better!

Naaman rushed back to Elisha's house. This time, Elisha himself came out to meet him.

'The God of Israel has made me well!' Naaman cried. 'No one else could help me. Now I know that the only true God is *your* God, Elisha.'

Naaman obeyed God at last – and God made a new friend.

How did Naaman make God happy?

Pens Prayer

Dear God, the only true God – thank You for being my best Friend. Amen.

Day 16 — GOD'S INVITATION

'God looks down from heaven … to see if there are any … who worship him.' (Psalm 53 v 2)

Diving with Gordon

Max told Marco.
Marco told Charlotte.
Charlotte told Denzil.
Denzil told Philipp[a]

'Guess what?' said Philippa, 'Gordon Gluestick has invited us all to go out on his boat! He's taking us diving in the sea! Isn't it exciting? We've all said yes, we'd love to go. Shall I tell Gordon you're coming, too?'

Gloria thought, 'I'm not sure I want to go diving. I'll get cold in the sea and the salt water will make a mess of my hair.'

So Gloria said, 'Don't worry, Philippa. I'll answer Gordon's invitation myself.'

But Gloria didn't.

Just as Pens have an invitation from Gordon, so we have an invitation from God. He wants us to share our lives with Him.

And then Philippa told Gloria.

Is Gloria doing the right thing or the wrong thing when she doesn't answer Gordon's invitation?

Pens Prayer

Thank You, Father God, for loving me so much that You invite me to share my life with You. Amen.

Day 17 — God's Invitation

'When you said, "Come and worship me," I answered, "I will come, LORD …"' (Psalm 27 v 8)

Gloria says no

Marco was SO excited about going diving that he couldn't stop bouncing!

He bounced out of bed.

He bounced downstairs for breakfast.

He bounced to see Max.

'Diving is going to be FANTASTIC, Max!' Marco beamed. 'I'm so glad we're all going.'

'I'm not sure it will be *all* of us,' replied Max. 'Gloria hasn't answered Gordon's invitation yet.'

So Marco bounced round to Gloria's house.

'No, I don't think I can go, Marco,' said Gloria. 'I'm going to be VERY busy that day.'

But Gloria wasn't going to be busy. She just didn't want to go diving.

> When God invites us to be His friends, He hopes we'll say yes.

> Have you ever had an invitation? What was it for?

Pens Prayer

You are the Lord of heaven and earth! Thank You, dear God, for wanting to be my Friend. Amen.

Day 18 — God's Invitation

'… be concerned above everything else with the Kingdom of God …' (Matthew 6 v 33)

Very important things

'I wish you were coming diving, Gloria,' sighed Charlotte.

'So sorry,' Gloria said. 'But I have very important things to do. They won't get done by themselves.'

'I could help,' suggested Charlotte. 'Then the very important things would get done twice as quickly. Would *that* give you time to come diving?'

'I'm afraid not,' Gloria replied. 'They are very important things that only I can do.'

Charlotte looked sad.

But Gloria thought, 'Why would I want to go diving anyway? I shall sit in my garden in the sunshine, and read a good book.'

Let's not be selfish. Let's spend time with our friends and with God.

How can you spend time with God?

Pens Prayer

Lord God, You always have time for me. I want to spend time with You, too. Amen.

Day 19 — God's Invitation

'Come near to God, and he will come near to you.' (James 4 v 8)

Rain

40

In the morning, on Pens' diving day, Gloria pulled back her curtains.

The sun wasn't shining. It was pouring with rain!

'Bother!' Gloria thought. 'Now I shan't be able to sit in my garden and read a good book.'

Then she spotted her Pens friends. They were running excitedly past her garden gate.

'They must be going to meet Gordon Gluestick,' Gloria said to herself. 'I suppose the rain doesn't matter when you're diving. You get wet anyway. Well, I'm glad *I'm* not going out in the rain. I can stay inside where it's warm and dry.'

God wants to be friends with everyone. Don't miss out on the adventure!

What do you like better? Playing in water, or keeping dry?

Pens Prayer

Thank You, Father God, for inviting me to join in Your adventure. Amen.

Day 20 — God's Invitation

'… [God] wants everyone to be saved and to come to know the truth.' (1 Timothy 2 v 4)

Splosh!

When they saw Gordon and Stubbs, Pens waved.

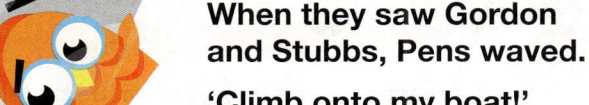

'Climb onto my boat!' grinned Gordon. 'Then put on your wetsuits.'

The wetsuits were special rubber clothes to keep Pens warm in the water. There was even a wetsuit for Sharpy.

Gordon started the boat's engine and they chugged out to sea.

When they stopped, Gordon helped Pens to strap tanks full of air onto their backs. They could breathe in the air under water through their masks.

'Let's dive!' said Gordon – and into the sea they went! SPLOSH! …

Back in Pens' town, Gloria had nothing to do.

It was still raining.

God feels sad about people who don't belong to His fam

Gloria's missing the diving fun. How do you think she feels at home on her own?

Pens Pray

Dear Lord, You are Father in heaven. be in Your family

Day 21 — God's Invitation

'God, who does not lie, promised us [eternal] life …'
(Titus 1 v 2)

Under the Sea

There was a whole new world under the sea. It was full of colours and wonderful creatures!

Max and Sharpy met an octopus. Charlotte smiled at a sea horse. Philippa waved at a crab. Denzil said hello to a starfish. Marco didn't know what to look at first. There was so much to see!

'Wow!' Marco thought. 'Look at all the different sea creatures! The world down here is beautiful.'

Gloria was missing the beautiful world under the ocean. All she could see out of her window was the grey sky, still full of rain.

When we say yes to God's invitation, we can enjoy a new life with Him forever.

How many legs does an octopus have?

Pens Prayer

Father God, thank You that You've promised that I can be with You always. Amen.

Day 22 — God's Invitation

'… if you search for [God] with all your heart, you will find him.' (Deuteronomy 4 v 29)

Shipwreck!

46

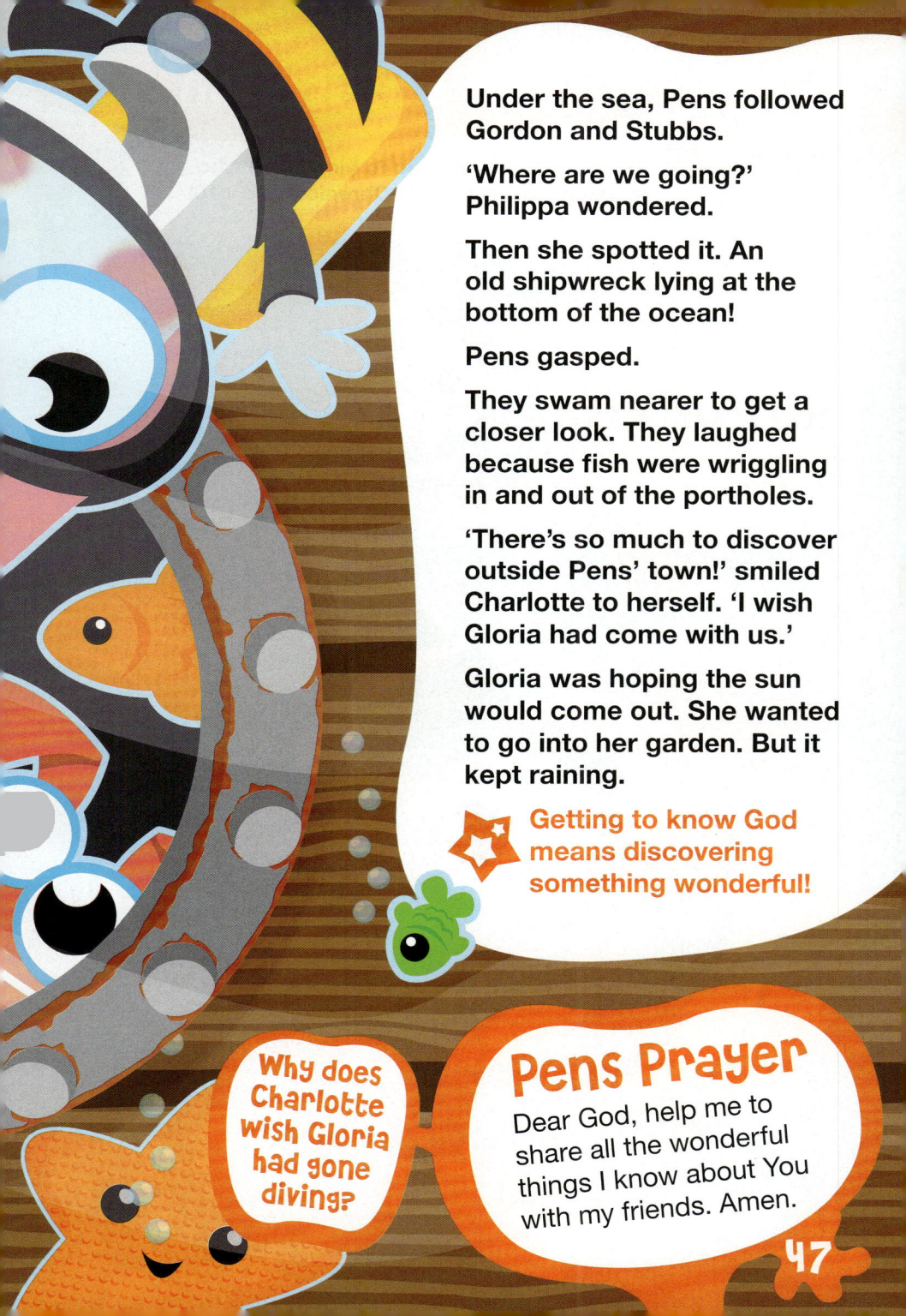

Under the sea, Pens followed Gordon and Stubbs.

'Where are we going?' Philippa wondered.

Then she spotted it. An old shipwreck lying at the bottom of the ocean!

Pens gasped.

They swam nearer to get a closer look. They laughed because fish were wriggling in and out of the portholes.

'There's so much to discover outside Pens' town!' smiled Charlotte to herself. 'I wish Gloria had come with us.'

Gloria was hoping the sun would come out. She wanted to go into her garden. But it kept raining.

Getting to know God means discovering something wonderful!

Why does Charlotte wish Gloria had gone diving?

Pens Prayer

Dear God, help me to share all the wonderful things I know about You with my friends. Amen.

Day 23 — God's Invitation

'Be glad that we belong to him; let all who worship him rejoice!' (1 Chronicles 16 v 10)

A shiny surprise

Gordon was swimming with Pens back to his boat.

Suddenly, he stopped.

In front of them was a dolphin! She was shiny and silvery. She seemed to be smiling at them.

Gordon held out his hand. The dolphin swam forwards and touched him with her nose.

Pens couldn't help laughing. The dolphin looked as if she might be laughing, too!

She swam over Pens. She swam under Pens.

Then she flicked her tail and glided away.

Pens beamed happily. Their day had been full of surprises.

But stay-at-home Gloria had enjoyed no surprises at all.

When God is our Friend, life is full of surprises!

What could you do to give someone a lovely surprise this week?

Pens Prayer

Loving Lord, thank You for all the good things in my life. Amen.

Day 24 — God's Invitation

'Listen! I stand at the door and knock; if anyone hears my voice and opens the door, I will come into his house …' (Revelation 3 v 20)

Gloria's Wish

'Thank you SO much, Gordon and Stubbs!' cried Pens when they got home from their diving expedition. 'That was the best day ever!'

The next morning, they all went to see Gloria. They couldn't wait to tell her about their adventure.

'I expect it was very cold, though,' muttered Gloria.

'We wore special rubber suits,' smiled Denzil. 'We didn't notice the cold.'

'Still,' Gloria replied, 'it must have been dark and dingy under the sea.'

'No!' beamed Denzil. 'It was BEAUTIFUL!'

'We're so pleased we said yes to Gordon's invitation,' added Philippa.

Gloria wished she'd said yes, too.

God invites us to be with Him forever. Let's say yes today.

What do you suppose Gloria will say next time Gordon invites Pens to go diving?

Pens Prayer

Father God, please share every day with me. Thank You. Amen.

A GREAT FEAST

Who's coming to the party?

Day 25

'There was once a man who was giving a great feast …' (Luke 14 v 16)

Party time!

Jesus wanted people everywhere to know how much God loved them.

He wanted them to hear God's invitation: 'Come and be My friends today.'

He wanted everyone to answer: 'Yes, God.'

So Jesus told a story. It was about a man who held a huge party. The man invited lots of people. He made sure there was plenty to eat and plenty to drink. At last everything was ready.

'Off you go now,' the man said to one of his servants. 'Go and tell my guests that it's party time!'

Jesus told people about God's invitation.

What party games do you know?

Pens Prayer

Thank You, Lord Jesus, that when I believe and trust in You, I can be close to God forever. Amen.

A Great Feast
Who's coming to the party?

Day 26

'But [his guests] all began, one after another, to make excuses.' (Luke 14 v 18)

'No!'

Off the servant went to find the invited guests.

'They'll be so excited when I tell them it's party time,' he thought to himself. 'Who wouldn't want to go to a brilliant party like this?'

When he saw the first guest, the servant smiled, 'It's time to get ready. The party's about to start!'

But the guest didn't smile. The guest didn't look happy at all.

'Ah, well,' he said, shaking his head. 'I can't possibly go to the party now. I've just bought a field and must go and look at it right away. Very sorry.'

God invites people to be His friends, but sometimes they make excuses and say no.

What sort of excuses do people make when they don't want to do something?

Pens Prayer

Father God, You love me so much. I love You, too. Amen.

A Great Feast
Who's coming to the party?

Day 27

'I have bought five pairs of oxen and am on my way to try them out …' (Luke 14 v 19)

'Very sorry'

The servant was puzzled.

'I thought everyone would be excited about the party,' he said to himself. 'But the man I've just spoken to doesn't want to go.'

So, he went to talk to another invited guest.

'It's time to get ready,' the servant smiled. 'The party's about to start!'

But the guest didn't smile. The guest didn't look happy at all.

'Ah, well,' he said, shaking his head. 'I can't possibly go to the party now. I've just bought some cows for my farm. I need to go and see how they're getting on. Very sorry.'

God is sad when people can't be bothered with Him.

How can you show God that you love Him?

Pens Prayer

Dear Lord, I'm sorry for the times when I forget to show You that I love You. Amen.

A Great Feast
Who's coming to the party?

Day 28

'I have just got married, and for that reason I cannot come.' (Luke 14 v 20)

more excuses

58

The servant frowned.

'How odd,' he thought. 'Now someone else doesn't want to go to the party.'

So, he went to find another invited guest.

'It's time to get ready,' the servant smiled. 'The party's about to start!'

But the guest didn't smile. The guest didn't look happy at all.

'Ah, well,' he said, shaking his head. 'I can't possibly go to the party now. I've just got married. Very sorry.'

The servant felt sorry, too. Everywhere he went, invited guests shook their heads. His master was throwing a wonderful party – but none of them wanted to go.

God invites us to a wonderful party, too – an amazing life with Him.

How would you feel if you invited your friends to a party and they all said no?

Pens Prayer

Loving God, thank You for inviting me to Your party. I love being close to You. Amen.

A Great Feast
Who's coming to the party?

Day 29

'The master … said to his servant, "Hurry out … and bring back the poor, the crippled, the blind, and the lame."' (Luke 14 v 21)

New invitations

The servant went back to his master sadly.

'I'm very sorry,' he said. 'I've told your invited guests that it's party time. But they're not coming. They all seem to have other things to do.'

The servant's master was very cross.

'If my guests can't be bothered to come to my party, then we'll find people who can. Go back out,' he said to his servant. 'Find people who are poor. Find people who are ill. Find people who can't walk or can't see. People no one cares about. Let's invite them to my party instead.'

God invites everyone to share their lives with Him – no matter who they are.

What could you do with your friends this week?

Pens Prayer

Thank You, Lord God, for all my friends. Please help me to be a good friend to them. Amen.

A Great Feast
Who's coming to the party?

Day 30

'How happy are those who will sit down at the feast in the Kingdom of God!' (Luke 14 v 15)

The fantastic party

Once more, the servant went to find people to go to the party. He invited poor people and ill people; those who couldn't walk and those who couldn't see. Just as his master had told him to.

They all said yes. But there was room for even more!

'Then go into the countryside,' the master said to his servant. 'Invite people from there, too. I want my house to be full of those who want to be here.'

In the end the house was full. Completely full!

And the guests who couldn't be bothered to go missed a fantastic party.

At God's party, there's room for everyone.

Have you ever been to a fantastic party? What did you enjoy the most?

Pens Prayer

Yes, Father God, I want to be Your friend and to come to Your party! Praise You! Amen.

Pens for special times.

An exciting short story plus 5 days of Bible-reading notes

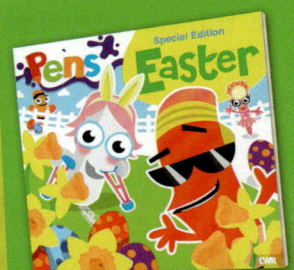

by Alexa Tewkesbury
32-page full colour booklets, 148x148mm and as animated downloads

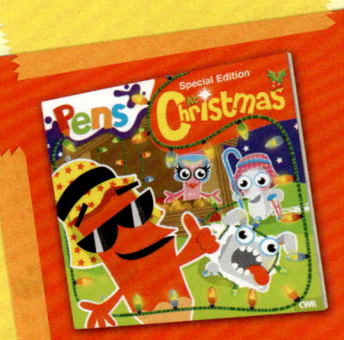

Easter
Help young children understand the true meaning of Easter.

Christmas
The *Pens* characters tell the Christmas story to make Jesus' birth real and memorable for young children.

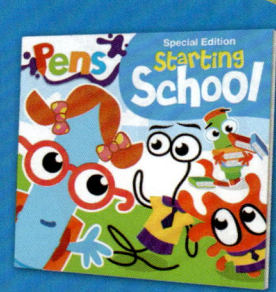

Starting School
Help children start school confidently, knowing that God goes there with them.

Available online, or from Christian bookshops.

For current prices or for animated downloads visit **www.cwr.org.uk/store**